More praise for *Unfoldings*

The poems of *Unfoldings* invite – and dare – us to inhabit complicated spaces: the tropes, myths, and tales we're fed and which poison us; the identities we occupy and which bind us to others, for bad and good; and the types of love that stand as antidote to the hard facts of living. Ronderos' explorations, across numerous themes, are as brave as her humanity is luminous.
— **Danielle Legros Georges**, Poet Laureate, City of Boston, 2015-2019

In *Unfoldings*, Clara Eugenia Ronderos creates a persona whose identity is always multiple, often straddling some world in and between the rough and tumble of lived experience and the less-than-idyllic truths of western fairy tales. In the sensibility that informs these brilliant poems, ideal and actual worlds meld together, sometimes undercutting one another, always informing each other. In the paradox of the self these poems celebrate, truth (like love) is always tough, unfolding, never singular, always multitudinous.
— **Stephen Haven**, Author of *The Last Sacred Place in North America*

Unfoldings

Collected Poems

CLARA EUGENIA RONDEROS

Nixes Mate Books
Allston, Massachusetts

Copyright © 2022 Clara Eugenia Ronderos

Book design by d'Entremont
Cover photograph used with permission.

All rights reserved. This book or any portion thereof may not be reproduced or used in any manner whatsoever without the express written permission of the publisher except for the use of brief quotations in a book review or scholarly journal.

ISBN 978-1-949279-42-9

Nixes Mate Books
POBox 1179
Allston, MA 02134
nixesmate.pub

Me gustaría
que me oyeras la voz y yo pudiera
oír la tuya.

Sí, sí hablo contigo
mirada silenciosa que recorre estas líneas

I would like you
to hear my voice, wish
I could hear yours.

Yes, yes, I am talking to you,
silent gaze
that runs over these lines

— Circe Maya / Jesse Lee Kercheval

To Mary. G. Berg who gifted me with an English voice
and an invaluable friendship.

Contents

On a Grown Woman's stilts

Concealed	3
Memories	5
Once upon a time	6
Manifesto against nobility	8
Cycles of desire	9
Obedience	11
Forbidden task	13
Daring	15
Changing routines?	16
From this side of the mirror	18
Identity issues	19
Paradox and self	21
The impostor	22

Unfoldings

Unfoldings	25
Of kings and Fortune	27
Low Tide	30

Seduction	31
Wedding poem	32
Transformations	33
Evening	35
Our daily bread	36
The Will	37

The many versions of its madness

Greenhouse	39
Chronicle	40
Training	42
A moment	43
Before the Wall Falls	44
Bends	45
Oedipus	46
Creation	47
The same river	48
The poet's visit	49
After history	50
Variations on blindness	52

A bridge bereft of riverbanks

Outside the fortress	55
Exile	56
Foreign Language	57
Two Passports	59
Avatar	61
The North	63
To My Cup of Coffee	65
Variations for a Wintry Day	66
Nosotros: USA	70
Acknowledgments	74
About the Author	77

Unfoldings

On a Grown Woman's stilts

Concealed

Beneath the house,
hiding inside her cave,
lives the girl who is afraid of light.
The fragile, hidden girl
grows inside her grey vault,
its spiral staircase
blocked by trap doors, flush with the ceiling,
flush with the floor.
Slow, slimy spiral,
always slippery, so she cannot
climb up,
get out,
let her amphibian eyes
bear the colors green and blue,
her thick blood,
bear red,
her skin, at last,
all of her translucent,
vulnerable and musty parchment-dry skin

become infused with light.

Inside her vaulted gray mansion
the girl sleeps now.

Memories

Mornings, like warm basins,
mornings of mashed fruits and broken stems
of flowers.
For how long, in the muddy hollow of my afternoons,
will your lingering time stand still,
mother,
and your distance
of words without skin, upon my flesh?

Once upon a time

You thought that milk and bread
came from the corner store
and that all would be ease and joy
like in a fairy tale.

You thought diapers were white and never stained
and that the garden and the kitchen
would have to obey the abracadabra of the white dress
reflected in the mirror
and in the camera's glass.
"...and they lived happily..." summarized
the story that you were just beginning.

(the swollen belly hidden under the veil
and the nausea after the champagne
said, maybe not.)

Said that the king would want to rule
over your palace
and that the marvelous spinners

would leave you with the impossible task of straw and gold,
and that your deformed lip and your gigantic thumb
and your foot would carry the weight
of that yearning for king and kingdom
that dragged you there.

The palace door has closed.
The guards are sleeping off their drunkenness
(in the kitchen or in the back patio,
exiled princess, you rue the day)

The milk gone sour and thick
and the moldy bread demand your care
and the indelible stain and the white nights without silence
and you, so innocent to think...

Manifesto against nobility

Only an authentic princess could have had such delicate skin

I wasn't a real princess
I didn't have a pea under my mattress
but rather a dragon that roared
and a pile of stones
and a melon.
I could sleep like a log
rocked by the hot breath
of the ferocious jaws,
my waist adjusted
with incredible grace
to the round shape of the melon.
No. I wasn't a real princess
delicate and happy
nor was my master a prince.
My skin was hardened leather,
my blood not blue at all.

On a stormy night
I walk outside again.

Cycles of desire

Even Little Red Riding Hood already knew
about the wolf
about his sharp and precise fangs
about his claws.

I, who've found him lurking,
even now, I cannot uncover him.
I converse with him among the flowers,
red with desire, he carries me off
to his lair.

I don't recognize his grandma disguise
I don't see huge ears hidden under his white cap.
Ferocious and alluring on the path,
behind the tree, in the bed.
I'm blind.
Only when I feel his icy ivory upon my neck,
the tell-tale claw under the softest skin,
do I run.

Armed with a shotgun,
comes the woodcutter-savior,
who kills the beast
and quickly is transformed
into a grandma with huge eyes, and hands and teeth.

Little Red Riding Hood in the closet, I wait.

Obedience

She was so disgusted by that cold creature
that she didn't even dare to touch it.

Gold ball rolls from the small hand to the well.
Noble frog traps round projectile,
in hope.
You shall give me your supper and your bed
my viscous green skin on your pillow.
(the little girl doesn't want him, the little girl doesn't see him)

In the castle of Ruben Darian luxury,
they dine.
The heavy cedar door barely shakes,
someone knocks.
You shall give me your supper and your bed
my viscous green skin on your pillow.
(the little girl doesn't want him, the little girl doesn't see him)

On a golden plate, huge eyes, feet,
a tongue unrolling like a rug over the table cloth

calls for justice.
You shall give me your supper and your bed
my viscous green skin on your pillow.
(the little girl doesn't want him, the little girl doesn't see him)

The father king, authority commanding over all,
demands unavoidable explanations. Obedient,
the girl speaks.
You shall give him your supper and your bed
his viscous green skin on your pillow.
(no, the girl doesn't want him, no, the girl doesn't see him)

Frog that takes what he wants from your plate,
prince in your bed to demand that you pay the price
for the golden ball.
You've already given him your supper and your bed
his viscous green skin on your pillow.
(no one wants the girl, no one sees the girl)

Forbidden task

*And she took the spindle and
wanted to spin, too.*

One hundred years of sleep turned into a bad habit:
Beauty has stopped spinning
and now awakes.
Blessed was she among all, graces piled upon her birth,
now cursed in the transgression of learning
an old-woman-in-the attic's trade. Beauty,
so many broken promises,
with one hundred years she paid for her defiance
(eyes closed and lips half open
waiting for the fatal kiss).

Beauty, on her stone bed,
waited…
Images from dreams interconnected by
one hundred years of desire
flowed out into a single kiss,
that, like that of Judas,

would sell her to the highest bidder
or prince
for his personal use.

She waited…
to fall into a stranger's hands,
another terrible bed
in which, as a guest,
her beautiful body became a
renewed curse
in insomnia and pain,
a thread to be twisted and spun,
never a hand that spins.

Beauty is awake
and the others seem to sleep.

Daring

From her mouth had sprung
the rock-hard diamond stone,
a red-black fairytale-like ruby
and a magnificent fragrant flower.
She was the good one, who gave drink to the thirsty,
the beautiful mistreated princess
with white skin, small feet, and a thick golden braid.
She, the bearer of silence.

The ugly, strong, dark skin,
like a scaly serpent under an Edenic apple tree,
she wanted to call everything by its proper name,
but horror whistled between her lips,
for toads and snakes would emerge from that mouth
because she dared to drink
the pure water from the well.

Changing routines?

Her skin was as white as snow,
her lips as red as blood and
her hair as black as a raven's wing.

Lips as red as blood
thickening as she waits beneath the gaze of another's desire.
White and cold and still
as snow, the skin
that buries her in its garment.
Black hair that flies toward death
gathered into braids or twists,
clipped bird's wings,
silenced by the combs and the crown.
That's how you were, my sad Snow White
when you'd furiously cleaned
the tiny house of the eunuch dwarves awaiting
the prince with the blazing sword,
with his horse impatient to gallop bearing your weight;
the prince, the only one able

to take you away from the seven
little sweaty beds,
from the seven greasy little plates,
and the seven screechy voices
that sang to you at night;
that blue prince, his blood blue with lassitude and loneliness
who desires your red to suck the juice
and bite the apple stuck in your throat.
That's how you were, pathetic, waiting
red and white and black,
beautiful Snow White.

From the little house in the woods to the palace,
the horse steps firmly as it takes you
to seven beds of gold with feathers,
to seven silver plates and seven voices who ask and demand
that you make the beds and wash the plates
and sing a lullaby before they sleep.

From this side of the mirror

She looked at pieces of her face in the mirror.
The hooded eye, the light down over the upper lip,
Cyrano's nose...
They didn't add up to much,
maybe nothing.
It was a mirror with edges, sharp,
who told her that, amongst all women,
the other one was better,
while rivers of blood ran
through the lines in her hands.

She
who didn't even have a poisoned apple
or a delayed white rabbit to help her
go
to the other side.

Identity issues

Why be a woman, not a person,
living being, character, neutral I inhabiting the earth
as any other I,
hermaphrodite? Capable of being
her or him
who sleeps and eats
and works to earn her sweat
her pride, her lofty brow?
Why withered and white
like Alfonsina, in the depths of the sea?
Why Virginia, her pockets full of rocks?
Why Clara and opaque
and not, it's clear that I exist and here I am in this world
where I belong?
Mother not father,
with my own keyhole without keys,
like Delmira who did, in spite of this, open the door.
A woman, standing on this earth
to live my life

like my body, like
my odd way of banging my head against the world
and giving shape to mud from my single borrowed rib.

Paradox and self

How do you keep your balance atop a furious steed,
upon the slight thin cord you navigate?

Grace and strength. Power and elegance.
Woman, who sleeps like a wild beast,
awakens like a lady, or an angel, or a princess.

How can you be the very same one who roars her desires?
She who takes by the hand an eternal helpless child?
You, tormented foam beating against cliffs,
a lake mirroring slow moving clouds
as they travel to no fixed destination?
How can you, yourself, be so much,
walking on a tight rope
with your ridiculous little parasol
and mighty enough to terrify the lion tamer?

The impostor

The little girl is scared
standing tall now on a grown woman's stilts
fooling everyone.
They don't see that beneath her cloak's
disguising creases,
she's a fearful and forgotten child.
But there she is hiding under her coat
that barely protects her from pain.
It bulks her out ("I'm filled out") she tells herself
so that no one can guess her secret.

And she moves cautiously
and speaks guardedly
and gazes as if from the depths of a well
hardly revealing her clumsiness,
evident
and easily taken for poise or wisdom.
Fear covered over;
guilt beneath her hat brim;

gloved hands that cannot or will not
grab hold.

Ripped apart,
exhausted by standing on tiptoe to seem
taller.

Unfoldings

Unfoldings

Rock bodies
paper bodies
metallic bodies
malleable under fire,
clay molded
into sculptures of pleasure.
Bodies, fallen down buildings,
sheets and shadows
secure their dreams.
Bodies, jails
to rebellious appetites
trapped within limits
of muscle and bone.
Sometimes they're graves
hiding treasures
forever silenced.
Sometimes magnets
attracting from behind veils,
hunters.

Or sometimes the body,
a spider web
where enemies
are trapped.

Of kings and Fortune

In your hand you held the lucky deck.
No doubt about it. The radical change
the fortune teller had foreseen that afternoon
was evident on the faces of those
playing-card monarchs,
righteous kings.
Diamonds and hearts, she'd said,
symbolize not only love and wealth but also the glow
and deep intuition of hidden truths.
A king of spades, forgotten now under the random pile
of worthless cards, had given way to the blond red king, in his
carnival splendor.
The melancholy smile of that dark king had been silenced
and the chords of a rhythm that you did not yet know
marked a new dancing-beat to your days.
It was finally the time of Happiness;
the kind of happiness suddenly surging from a spell
of mice that trot pulling a carriage

You looked at your face in the mirror,
your out of control smile,
and you hoped to find the princess,
the protagonist of the novel you haven't written,
the little girl you mutilated when you hid her little notebook of poems...
They had abandoned you
and you felt like you were all alone.

But the king,
(you soon found out)
had no power over them
over any of them.
You had to strangle him, clip his triumphant K into bits,
senselessly shear his ancient beard,
cut him up and put him back together again
to place
        his heart in your chest
                his diamonds in your bag
                        his scepter barricading your door.

Then you opened your hand to let
the beheaded kings
of your destiny
fall.

Low Tide

This morning the sea roars with silent fury
and the sand wears a festive bullfighter's suit.
The music of accordions
steeps in the salty swaying
of the breeze
and I am happy.
Lost in disorder, covered by salt and light,
by that which is not me
and is everything when it blends with me
this morning, I smile
shaken
by the coming and going of the sea.

Swollen sail
amid an immense quiet
from which the full roundness of the horizon
can be seen.

Seduction

Fortress, menaced by foam.
Like a game.
It comes and goes,
then returns with a thousand faces,
with veils, with luster.
Splintering the sun, it takes away tiny grains.
Then, rushing into the moat, creates another moat,
undermining the structure,
rocking it.
Sleepy, it abandons itself to the white jaws
its body soft, green
now, salty and translucent.

Wedding poem

How difficult the love
that tastes of daily bread.
Love of home and blankets,
of the grocery bag for the marketplace.

Love that is chained but not condemned,
an "I love you", unwavering until death,
like a mountain forever towering
and lonely. Solid in its stillness:
little intricate paths run through it,
like deep scars.

It remains motionless, always,
even when fire roars within it,
when cascades and green buds sprout from its skin.

This is the only one;
the tough and true love,
unexplored by the silver screen;
seldom, have I seen its cloudy peak
emerging from a library shelf.

Transformations

Those days were easy days of fire
when pressing matters mattered most.
Those days the two of us were one,
not even that, sometimes,
a body with no heads, no feet to run.
Those days were easy days of fire.

Our days are full of smoke these days,
we cough in dissonance, we snore,
the two of us are clearly two or more:
one that remembers while wanting to forget
another that forgets keys, names and codes,
a third one floats in nothingness as time goes by.
Our days are full of smoke these days.

This morning was a time of rain and storm,
we talked for hours, we let it rip and roar.
We were as many as we have ever been;
the one who yells, the one who listens and denies,
the one who argues beyond doubt,

and then condemning slams the door and cries.
This morning was a time of rain and storm.

Evening

Love and night are the remedy
to all the evils on the face of the Earth.
Love wraps misery inside its quilt
when night lies down beneath the tired sun.
On her knees, night produces through all her mouths
filled with light, a prayer to calm your spirits
and soften the rocks that weighed heavily
inside the belly of the afternoon.
And the arms, and the legs and the teeth of love,
in that well of silent tranquility
wade, and kick and bite the pain.

Night and love, the only compassion in the face of absurdity.

Our daily bread

I no longer have words of love to give
only worn out and tired images return to us
like little horses in an ancient merry go round zoo.

No novel ways to touch, no tricks, no affectations.
I have only what I am and what we give each other
in the bed we share, drinking our morning coffee.

I just tell you stories of things that happen daily
known to you, or imagined, no surprises;
the past no longer split in fearsome bifurcations.

But a miracle is renewed
in this peace, in this hand that knows your hand,
in this body, casually stretching.

A closed-eyed and silent pleasure
of memories and small triumphs
belongs to this unadorned love

so tame and sober.

The Will

What happens if you die before me?
He says.
What happens if I live beyond your years?
She responds.
And then they turn to numbers.
They add and multiply
as if the pain they fear could be contained
in hidden sums.

Until one of them is gone
and the other grieves
and counts, remembering the bickering
with regret
wishing for that sunny morning

when they had all the wealth.

The many versions of its madness

Greenhouse

This afternoon at five thirty
a poem
blooms in the silence of a library.
It frees itself from nonexistence
incontrovertible evidence
of a voice that slept
but is asleep no longer.
It spreads over the surface,
indelible mark of wounds
still unhealed.

(no spells have yet been found to heal them)

A minute later it dries up,
produces the hard shell that covers naked flesh
and only this rebellious trace
remains.

Chronicle

Thus life continued without pause,
the neighbor's pain like a splinter
in our own heart's history.
Failures of others multiplying like echoes
in the same dark tunnel
where our own failures were hiding,
almost forgotten.

A life of connected sad stories
like stars in a pitiless constellation
ruling over all destinies.
Bitter moments like dots connected by
the unknowing hand of a child
who, without understanding the overall design,
traces the story of a curse.

Thus continues life with its bang bang of war,
with its bruised purple mourning dress.
In slow rhythm, exasperating at times,
that later escalates to the madness of monotony.

Pain, pain, pain and grief
and the struggle to find what fades away.
Fleeting moments like sparklers,
bright, festive, inevitably end
in twisted black wires
refuse of the brief splendor.

Thus I saw life go on unpunished and so shameless.
Thus I stayed afloat
inside my small dungeon of words.

Training

It was like riding a bicycle
a skill you never forget.
But in practice...
Tipping over on turns, losing control when braking,
a hollow in your stomach when going downhill.
And going uphill on foot.

It was like swimming
which you never forget.
But in practice...
The water seems colder and hostile when you are back,
keeping afloat with a drowner's little kicks
while you recover a dolphin's grace and agility.

It was like dying
you learn it as a child
and you never forget.
But in practice...

A moment

Poetry in the blood
rushing through narrow conduits
in search of a heart.
A red torrent
feeding tissues
feeding skin
vulnerable
envelope
for poetry and blood.

It pulses
to gush out
to spill
onto the page
where a heart
might find it.

Before the Wall Falls

May has reached
this corner of the garden.
Only a flowering branch
triumphs over the frost,
only one bird on that stubborn branch.

May with its breeze and sun
misses the rest of my frozen garden;
its happy voice is lost in the glacial echo
of blasts of wind speckled with white.

May has arrived
awaited on dark gray days
on nights that extended comfortably.

A greater silence in that lone bird, intense cold
when the branch flares out in the corner.
Its imprudent joy erupts in the garden
of gigantic egotism where I live abandoned
by the complete blaze and tumult
of true springtime.

Bends

The days traveled by horse and buggy,
slow clicketyclack producing
sleepiness.
Suddenly,
the wheel tires of mud
loud grumbling breaks out in what was a cradle.
Then days are harnessed up in anger
their trotting rocks violently
dragons pulling,
there is fire.
Those days
turn into wounds.
They, too, are slow
and sleepless.

Oedipus

Others might know the answer
to this riddle
I know the many versions of its madness
the multiplying questions
I know the silent Sphynx and the irony
of her quiet stare.
Others might look at her and laugh
because they know better

not me.

Again I breathe with difficulty
my stomach in a knot
my eyes fixed on her eyes
and not a word comes out.

Then her mouth opens
only to reveal

a new riddle.

Creation

Words weigh heavy inside me
trapped
between chest and back.

They fall like enormous fruit
losing their shape
as they abruptly
land with a crash.

The same river

Now I see clearly
there's no marching backward.
The path snakes along deceptively
as if trained to confuse.
The bends look like returns
but they take the walker
even farther away.
The return is a mirage
of distance
forgetting change.

The only truth of its course
Heraclitus' river.

The poet's visit

Ours were similar paths
I told myself
and thus
we should be friends.
I looked for a keyhole
in your eyes
to unlock a smile,
for a wobbly tile
in that edifice of pride,
where my words
might seep.
I found no wounds,
no cracks for a fortuitous break-in.

I found the silver platter
the golden key
the jewel in your chest.

Its glitter broke like glass
the only wound was mine.

After history

> *Land has opened at the feet of Colombia*
> *and time has been unable to*
> *detain the march of liberty*
> — Simon Bolivar

Histories are written on the faces of many, not in the books that lie,
not in the useless archives where time devours yellowed paper
and reduces it to fine dust that makes you sneeze.
History is not in a stone chiseled by slaves
who tell their king's deeds
but in the sad face of the slaves' great grandchildren
begging for bread on street corners.
Bolivar's letters and his delirium
upon the always white top of the gigantic Chimborazo
say nothing about the history of these his liberated lands,
where dark faces wear permanent masks of pain,
where men like him still write their dreams,
printed in poverty and hunger and exile.

In the neighborhood, in the shop
where credit is needed to buy bit of chocolate,
in the plaza where the neighbors bargain
for a bruised orange and a *yuca*,
at the school gates where a boy waits for someone to open
one of the many doors usually slammed in his face,
in the countryside of broken backs and blackened hands,
there, history cries out its stories,
there, a war is written and a river of blood flows
through the text, that no one takes the trouble to read.

Variations on blindness

1

No one will know the agony
a boy walking
a handsome boy at that
no one will know there is a broken heart
inside.
His curly hair moves with the wind
he seems to smile
a frozen smile of fear to hold his strength
no one will know that's all it is
when this boy walks
from home to school
alone.

2

A woman enters the train
her children in tow
one

two
three
(other passengers count)
the one inside the womb they cannot see
the hunger in their hearts they cannot see
only their clothes they see and think
"What was she thinking? So many and so badly kept!"
Her bravery and strength they do not see.
She quietly walks to the end of the car
gently motioning her kids to follow
(other passengers stare and scorn)
she thinks "only a couple stops and then perhaps
I will let my children play in the park for a bit
while I sit on the bench and rest
invisible and free."

A bridge bereft of riverbanks

Outside the fortress

To own a language is to stretch and bend
the words,
a borrowed language lacks this elasticity
and grace.
To learn the game, takes double skill and fearlessness
and will
to touch the words like rocks and make them fly
like birds,
to sing the words like notes and have them flow
like air,
to make the foreign language speak as water
spills
takes years of silence and regret.

The need to speak.

Exile

I have two homelands: Cuba and the night. — José Martí

He had two homelands
and I none.
Borders, wounds,
deep trenches in which the spoken word
is silent in two languages,
are the home I lost.
A suitcase is where my dreams reside,
incomplete on both sides of the line.
A bed like a divided map
a dish of lentils in exchange for a birthright
an eternal window on a moving train,
this land gazes at me from afar.
Departing, arriving, from where to where?
Arriving, departing, mi casa/home/mi casa/home doesn't exist.
I'm a bridge bereft of riverbanks
I'm that bloody flower the passing poet
glimpsed on the black dress.

Ithaca no longer exists.

Foreign Language

Let's play the guessing game of the impossible word
that only you know you know.
Let's play the infinite game
of the missing name.
Yesterday I understood your words, today I fear them.
Your language has turned to poison,
its slow fumes ooze over my days,
over my nights.

Let's play Hopscotch,
you toss the stone, I hop on one foot
and I never reach Heaven.
Blind Man's Bluff is a good game, too;
blindfolded, I seek what I haven't lost,
you move around teasing me
and all I can find is a white wall
against which I always bash my head
my mouth and nose.
My soul.

You win, I lose.
That's how the game is. You know; I don't.
You give orders; I play, I dance
to the tune
of your flute.

Let's play, let's play, let's keep on playing.
Helter skelter,
higgledy piggledy,
let's play the impossible game
take it away here and add it there
stick your foot in and pull it back bitten
break your bones and lose your center
your turn that
you've already lost.

Two Passports

The plane,
the suitcase, fifty pounds exactly,
heading for life in that other place.

A last night's sleep on this side of the sea.
Tomorrow, in the mountains, where the sea is a myth
with many names.

The journey, planned months ago,
looms ahead like a wall
separating the cemetery
from a garden that seems like paradise.

A paradise whose only function is to expel.

Welcoming warmly, it embraces, retains for a month
the sunny green gaze of its visitor
who is then hurled back over the wall
back to the starting point
over there.

Over here, people work
to earn what we're doomed to spend,
we can dream of returning, we hope, we despair
and buy a new ticket, economy fare,
unrefundable, untransferable, obligatory
as light at the end of a tunnel
that never ends,
but is only regularly interrupted
by that pretense of belonging
by that leap of flight from tombs
by tomorrow's inevitable landing
year after year, surrounded
by darkness.

Avatar

Only science fiction
can explain
this coming and going
from mountains to flat
paved streets.

A silent body
stays behind, buried in deep sleep
as my plane lands
in that world of mine
where I am barely alive
and truly live.

Another body functions
in my own land
in the realm of fantasy,
it wins battles, climbs on clouds
amongst blue men and women,
it thrives.

But the blood-and-bones-body
must wake up.
The one making money and fulfilling tasks.
That one, after the trip, already unplugged,
only sees in tatters, the memory
of the other blue, happy body
now
figment
dream
nothing.

The North

In this weird country
I'm given too much food
and loneliness.
They give me too much sex
and loneliness.
Gold and heaped up treasures
and loneliness.
They supply me with names and numbers
and so much, for me, so much
loneliness they give me here.
And dreams to dream
they bring in loneliness
and offer paradise,
steam-pressured speed,
and loneliness.

They also
sell you
jars and labels

and recipes
for happiness.
You open them
without finding
anything other
than more of the same
lonely loneliness
given
to me and to you and me.

To My Cup of Coffee

(An elemental ode, in the style of Neruda, exercise for a literature class)

In the mornings
from your ardent mouth
to mine
black fire.
Bitter marvel
of my distant land.

Your blue walls were molded
by the potter's agile hands
and in your small belly
lives the warmth that begins the morning.
With a bit of bread, on my table,
you look like a small soldier
ready now to engage in another battle
in this black war of nightmares
that we undertake together
to overcome sleepiness.

Variations for a Wintry Day

1

Outside: snow and disorder
the cave hides me.
I was a tropical child
in a little dress of flowered cotton.
Wrapped in heavy cloth like drapes
I stay home today
contemplating the time
that has passed
just as the raging storm outside
will pass, as did the one
that used to rage in my
heart, now tender, flowering
within me.

2

What do you think now, mother,
of this, your daughter, as she traverses

this distant sunscape reverberating
on ice.
This professionally foreign daughter?
Hat, gloves, scarf
cover her from head to toe.
You no longer recognize her.
She was always strange, "bizarre", you'd say,
exotic now: caged bird,
her green color clashing in this white space
just as its pallor wept into your colors

of gray and black strength,
seamless solidity.

6

It sings out over the snow
as if spring had come,
ignoring what it sees.
Its shivering feathers
also ignore the cold,
it feels so compelled to sing.

8

I adore words, like goats on the run
I barely catch onto them as they race.
Like tame little domesticated animals
conforming to my desires.
I adore elusive words and
ones that scratch like wild cats
making skin bleed.
But I hate them when they are birds of prey
swooping onto whatever has fallen
and licking up the pain.
I hate them in the market and in fake jewels
when they tumble around falsely or shopworn.
I adore words and I fear them
because they hold everything,
even emptiness.
I respect words and it hurts me when they are trodden upon,
wounded, lame, blinded or murderous.

Rabbits pulled from a tophat, whales spouting their forceful crystal spray; round winged turtledoves,

the simplest sparrows of city parks.
I adore words that are startled, that fly up
and soar off.

Nosotros: USA

Todos se tapan con la misma manta
Adagio popular

Latinos, hispanos, latinoamericanos
Emigrados, chicanos, hispanoparlantes
o agringados
vivimos todos en tierra que nos desconoce;
Nos olvida aunque lavemos sus platos,
sirvamos su cena, eduquemos a sus hijos
desde la cuna.
Somos cobija de esfuerzos y desvelos
que reconoce sus tejidos.
En el counter de la aerolínea,
en la cafetería,
en la registradora de un almacén,
los hispano parlantes
los hispano sintientes
los hispano dolientes
nos reconocemos.

The all cover themselves with the same blanket
Popular saying

Latinos, hispanics, latinamericans ,
immigrants, chicanos, spanish-speakers
or gringoized
we all live in a land that disowns us
forgets us even when we do their dishes
serve their meals, educate their children
since birth.
We are a blanket of sleepless efforts
that recognizes its pattern.
At the airline counter
in the cafeteria
at the store's cash-register
the Spanish-speaking
the Spanish-feeling
the Spanish-aching
recognize each other

y un saludo amplio
anuda otra puntada
y nos sentimos parte de algo
que se nombra de tantas formas
y que no tiene, por lo tanto, nombre,
pero que corre de lado a lado de este territorio
inhóspito.
Hierba, yedra, florecida y múltiple forma de vida,
amable, alegre alharaca que resuena
a pesar de silencios impuestos
a pesar de olvidos,
a pesar..
ah pesar
compartido,
porque las penas con pan
son menos
pero no solo de pan
vive el hombre.

and an open greeting
weaves another line
and we feel part of something
named in so many different ways
and for that reason nameless,
running through this inhospitable territory,
end to end.
Grass, ivy, blooms, multiple forms of life
aimable, happy racket resounding
in spite of imposed silences
in spite of forgetfulness
in spite..
oh spite,
shared
because all sorrows with bread
are less
but man does not live
by bread alone.

Acknowledgments

Published in Spanish in 2012 as part of *Raiz del Silencio* by Clara Eugenia Ronderos. They were translated by Clara Eugenia Ronderos. These have never been published in English.
- Concealed
- Memories
- Issues of Identity
- Paradox of the Self

Published in *Metamorphoses* volume 18 Spring 2010 as Untitled. Translated by Mary G. Berg.
- The Impostor.

From *Después de la Fábula* by Clara Eugenia Ronderos. Madrid. Editorial Verbum. 2018 Translated by Mary G. Berg and Clara Eugenia Ronderos.
- Once Upon a Time
- Manifesto Against Nobility
- Cycles of Desire
- Obedience
- Forbidden Task

   Daring
   Changing Routines?
   From this Side of the Mirror
   The Same River
   After History

The poems: Cycles of Desire, Obedience, Forbidden Task and Changing Routines? Appeared in *Violence Against Women* 26 (14) 2020 1817-1822.

From *De reyes y fuegos* by Clara Eugenia Ronderos Madrid: Editorial Torremozas. 2018 , Translations by Clara Eugenia Ronderos and Mary G. Berg.
   Unfolding
   Of Kings and Fortune
   Low Tide
   Seduction
   Wedding Poem
   Evening
   Our Daily Bread

Two of these poems had appeared in English versión in: Ronderos, Clara Eugenia (2000) "Marea Baja / Low Tide," *mOthertongue*: Vol. 7 , Article 5. Available at: https://scholarworks.umass.edu/mot/vol7/

iss1/5 Ronderos, Clara Eugenia (2000) and "Seducción / Seduction," *mOthertongue*: Vol. 7, Article 13.

Poems from *Estaciones en exilio* Madrid: Torremozas 2010. An English version of these poems translated by Mary G. Berg and Clara Eugenia Ronderos appeared in *The Poetry of Clara Eugenia Ronderos Seasons of Exile*. New York: Mellen 2015. These are new versions revised by Clara Eugenia Ronderos

- Greenhouse
- Chronicle
- Training
- Before the Wall Falls
- Bends
- Exile
- Foreign Language
- Two Passports
- The North
- To my Cup of Coffee
- Variations for a Wintry Day

Other poems not included in this list were written in English in the original and have not been previously published.

About the Author

Clara Eugenia Ronderos, a Colombian-American poet and short-story writer, is a retired Professor of Spanish at Lesley University. Ronderos holds a Ph.D. in Hispanic Literature from University of Massachusetts Amherst. Her recent publications include *The Poetry of Clara Eugenia Ronderos: Seasons of Exile* Lewiston NY: Edwin Mellen Press, 2015, Mary. G. Berg's translation of her prize-winning collection *Estaciones en Exilio* (2010); as well as *Ábrete Sésamo*, Torremozas, Madrid: 2016 (short stories), *De Reyes y Fuegos*, Torremozas, Madrid: 2018 (poetry); *Después de la Fábula*, Verbum, Madrid: 2018 (poetry); and *Agua que no has de beber* (short stories) Alción, Córdoba, Argentina: 2019.

She currently lives between West Brookfield, Massachusetts and Subachoque, Colombia. Her location in rural settings in two different parts of the world informs much of her work in progress.

42° 19′ 47.9″ N 70° 56′ 43.9″ W

Nixes Mate is a navigational hazard in Boston Harbor used during the colonial period to gibbet and hang pirates and mutineers.

Nixes Mate Books features small-batch artisanal literature, created by writers who use all 26 letters of the alphabet and then some, honing their craft the time-honored way: one line at a time.

nixesmate.pub

www.ingramcontent.com/pod-product-compliance
Lightning Source LLC
Chambersburg PA
CBHW051807100526
44592CB00016B/2608